# Skills Builders

YEAR 6

## GRAMMAR AND PUNCTUATION

Sarah Turner

# Acknowledgements

Every effort has been made to trace all copyright holders, but if any have been inadvertently overlooked, the Publishers will be pleased to make the necessary arrangements at the first opportunity.

Although every effort has been made to ensure that website addresses are correct at time of going to press, Rising Stars cannot be held responsible for the content of any website mentioned in this book. It is sometimes possible to find a relocated web page by typing in the address of the home page for a website in the URL window of your browser.

Hachette UK's policy is to use papers that are natural, renewable and recyclable products and made from wood grown in sustainable forests. The logging and manufacturing processes are expected to conform to the environmental regulations of the country of origin.

ISBN: 978-1-78339-731-0



First published in 2016 by Rising Stars UK Ltd
Rising Stars UK Ltd, An Hachette UK Company
Carmelite House, 50 Victoria Embankment
London EC4Y 0DZ

www.risingstars-uk.com

All facts are correct at time of going to press.

Author: Sarah Turner
Educational Consultant: Madeleine Barnes
Publisher: Laura White
Illustrator: Emily Skinner
Logo design: Amparo Barrera, Kneath Associates Ltd
Design: Julie Martin
Typesetting: Newgen
Cover design: Amparo Barrera, Kneath Associates Ltd
Project Manager: Sarah Bishop, Out of House Publishing
Copy Editor: Hayley Fairhead
Proofreader: Jennie Clifford
Software development: Alex Morris



British Library Cataloguing-in-Publication Data
A CIP record for this book is available from the British Library.
Printed by Liberduplex S.L., Barcelona, Spain

# Contents

## GRAMMAR



## PUNCTUATION



All of the answers can be found online. To get access, simply register or login at **www.risingstars-uk.com**.

# Word classes

Different words do different jobs in a sentence. Words are divided into **word classes**: nouns, pronouns, verbs, adverbs, conjunctions, prepositions and determiners.

| Word class | Definition | Examples |
|---|---|---|
| **Nouns** | tell you the names of people, places, feelings and things | Rohit, Adrian, Manchester, chair, love |
| **Pronouns** | replace a noun to avoid repetition | **He** played on **his** scooter.<br>**That** is the best picture. |
| **Verbs** | tell you what is happening in a sentence | She **played** a game.<br>They **are going** to the swimming baths. |
| **Adverbs** | explain when, why or how an action happens | I stroked the dog **gently**. She won the match **yesterday**. |
| **Conjunctions** | connect words, phrases and clauses | Ruby brushed her teeth **before** she went to bed.<br>**If** it is raining tomorrow, we will need our umbrellas. |
| **Prepositions** | show the position of things | He put it **under** the chair.<br>**After** supper we went to bed. |
| **Determiners** | always placed before a noun and help to define it | **All** children love to play games.<br>**The** teacher read **a** book. |

## Activity 1

Circle the prepositions in the sentences below.

**a)** She waited until 10 o'clock.

**b)** It was after midday when the TV was fixed.

**c)** I bought some milk from the supermarket.

**d)** My sister sat by my mum on the bus.

## Activity 2

Circle the adverbs in the sentences below.

**a)** Excitedly, Dan opened the heavy lid. He paused briefly and looked at the treasure.

**b)** Quickly, the mouse ran through the small hole. She looked angrily at the cheese she had dropped.

**c)** Close the windows firmly, and securely lock the door.

**d)** "We will meet here after the party," she explained cheerfully.

**e)** He played excellently. He is clearly a skilled player.

## Activity 3

Which pair of pronouns is the best to complete the sentences below?

**a)** The teacher split _______ into teams. _______ were batting; the other team was fielding.

Tick **one** pair.

| | | |
|---|---|---|
| they | them | ☐ |
| us | we | ☐ |
| her | she | ☐ |
| them | I | ☐ |

**b)** The tins of beans were on such a high shelf that _______ had to ask someone to help _______.

Tick **one** pair.

| | | |
|---|---|---|
| he | him | ☐ |
| she | his | ☐ |
| they | our | ☐ |
| him | them | ☐ |

## Activity 4

Put the correct letter in each box to show what type of word it is pointing to.

**N = Noun** **P = Preposition** **D = Determiner** **V = Verb**

**a)** 

The baby hugged the cuddly toy in her pram.

**b)** 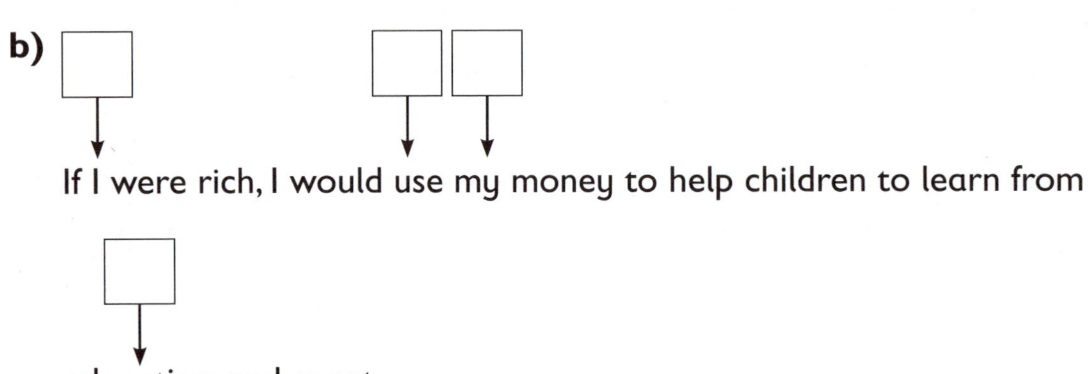

If I were rich, I would use my money to help children to learn from education and sport.

**c)** 

The lively puppy barked and chased its own tail enthusiastically.

**d)** 

She gave her brother a popular computer game for his birthday.

**e)** 

Alice sat between her best friend and her sister at the cinema.

## Activity 5

Use the tables below to identify the different word classes underlined in the sentences.

**a)** Alyssa plays netball on Tuesdays, but I think she is much better at crazy golf.

| Word | Verb | Adjective |
|---|---|---|
| plays | | |
| think | | |
| crazy | | |

**b)** Joshua carried the delicate chocolate egg carefully from the kitchen; however, Suzie ran past and knocked it out of his hands.

| Word | Verb | Noun | Adjective | Adverb |
|---|---|---|---|---|
| carried | | | | |
| delicate | | | | |
| egg | | | | |
| carefully | | | | |
| kitchen | | | | |
| ran | | | | |
| knocked | | | | |
| hands | | | | |

**c)** Sally eats sandwiches every day for her lunch although her mum wants her to try the delicious pasta salad she makes instead.

| Word | Verb | Noun | Adjective | Adverb |
|---|---|---|---|---|
| eats | | | | |
| sandwiches | | | | |
| mum | | | | |
| to try | | | | |
| delicious | | | | |
| pasta salad | | | | |

## Investigate!

Can you use some of the words in the activities to create a crossword with clues for others to complete?

# 2 Types of nouns

**Nouns** tell you the names of people, places, feelings and things. There are different types of nouns.

| **Proper nouns** | Names of people, places, times, occasions and events. | **Claire** and **Chris** got married in **England**. |
|---|---|---|
| **Common nouns** | The general name of things: animals, plants, objects. | He put the **plates** on the **table** near the **window**. |
| **Collective nouns** | Names given for groups of people, animals or other collections. | a **swarm** of bees<br>a **flock** of sheep<br>a **choir** of singers |
| **Abstract nouns** | Names of things you cannot see, such as feelings and ideas. | hate<br>happiness<br>truth |

## Activity 1

Underline the common nouns in blue and the proper nouns in red in the following sentences.

**a)** The house is on Main Street.

**b)** Katya played with her sister.

**c)** Dee went to the Manchester Pet Shop.

**d)** There were no yellow highlighters in the box.

**e)** Let's go and have a cheeseburger at Burger Bar.

## Activity 2

Add a noun to each of the following sentences or phrases.

### Common nouns

**a)** Rachel and Harriet threw the __________ back and forth across the playground.

**b)** Aaron was tired; he couldn't wait to get home and collapse on his __________.

**c)** Jemma packed all of her __________ into a big __________ so that she would be ready for her holiday the following morning.

### Proper nouns

**d)** I can't wait to start my new school today; it's called __________.

**e)** Kelly shouted across the field to her friend __________, but he didn't hear.

**f)** David and his family were on the plane, about to set off for__________.

### Collective nouns

**g)** A __________ of sheep.

**h)** A __________ of geese.

**i)** A __________ of whales.

**j)** A __________ of deer.

**k)** A __________ of foxes.

**l)** A __________ of locusts.

### Abstract nouns

jealousy trust honest anger love relaxation

**m)** Mel lets Sanjay put a blindfold on her and lead her to her surprise birthday present because they have a friendship that is full of __________.

**n)** Fatimah runs a bubble bath and puts candles all around the edge; she needs some __________ time.

**o)** A mother gives birth to a beautiful baby boy and cradles him; her heart is filled with __________.

### Investigate!

How many collective nouns can you find? Use the school library and the Internet to create the longest list possible.

# 3 Verbs

**Verbs** are words that describe an action, happening, process or state of being. A verb can change according to what or whom it refers. The **tense** of a verb indicates when the action happened.

An **action verb** tells what the subject of the sentence is doing.

jumped, walking, drinking, goes

- Marla **goes** to the magic show.

A **linking verb** connects the subject to a noun or adjective.

am, is, are, was, were

- Chloe and Ryan **were** the assistants at the magic show.

## Activity 1

Circle the linking verbs and draw a line under the action verbs.

**a)** Cole moved the washing machine into the house.

**b)** The goat kicked the barn door.

**c)** Miranda is my best friend.

**d)** Hurry! Climb over the wall!

**e)** Are you my new teacher?

## Activity 2

Copy these sentences. The verbs are all in the **present tense**. Underline each verb and write out the sentence again in the **past tense**. One has been done for you.

Peter <u>is drying</u> his face. Peter <u>dried</u> his face.

**a)** Sowmiya is reading a comic.

**b)** Joshua is playing his guitar.

**c)** Nurin is painting a picture.

**d)** Subinah is combing her hair.

## Investigate!

How many action verbs can you name in one minute? Try to beat your friend's score.

# 4 Subjunctive mode (mood)

The **subjunctive mode** is used for expressing hypothetical, wishful or imaginary situations. It can be used in commands and requests. It was an everyday part of Old English but is now rarely used. When we are wishing or imagining, we always use the word **were**.

If he **were** properly supervised, this would not have happened.

He wishes he was at the rugby.

I wish Kim was here as she would know the answer.

## Activity 1

Draw lines to complete these subjunctive sentences. The first one has been done for you.

| | |
|---|---|
| My teacher prefers that | if the weather is nice tomorrow. |
| It's advisable that you | keep the bandages on for a few days. |
| Tom suggested we go fishing | she apply to Oxford University. |
| Her maths teacher advised | travel plan before she goes away. |
| Mum insisted that Joanna make a | we meet twice a week. |

## Activity 2

Circle the correct option to complete these sentences.

**a)** Victor suggested that I (gets/got/get) more exercise.

**b)** They demanded that we (do not be/are not being/not be) so loud.

**c)** I recommend that you (look/looking/to look) for a job that isn't so stressful.

**d)** Nina asked that we (not disturb/did not disturb/are not disturb) her.

**e)** The weather reporter said it was advisable that we (taking/take/to take) an umbrella today.

## Investigate!

Can you find some examples in your reading books where the subjunctive mode has been used?

How would you use this in your writing?

# 5 Sentence types and question tags

Different types of sentences require different punctuation.

| | | |
|---|---|---|
| **Statements** | I saw a big, scary dog near the shops. | . |
| **Questions** | Do you know him?<br>Have you seen the film? | ? |
| **Commands** | Stop!<br>Wait!<br>Look out! | ! |

A **question tag** is a phrase added to the main part of the sentence, inviting the listener to confirm or give an opinion about the comment.

You have already seen the film, haven't you?

He will come today, won't he?

## Activity 1

Decide if these sentences are statements, commands or questions. Tick one box for each sentence.

a)

| | Statement | Command | Question |
|---|---|---|---|
| The film started on time. | | | |
| Switch it off! | | | |
| How long does the film last? | | | |
| The interval lasts for 20 minutes. | | | |
| When does the cinema close? | | | |

b)

| | Statement | Command | Question |
|---|---|---|---|
| Where is the aquarium? | | | |
| Fish live underwater. | | | |
| Stop touching the glass! | | | |
| How do fish breathe? | | | |
| Lunch is served in the café. | | | |

## Activity 2

Add a question tag to each of these sentences.

**a)** They are watching TV, ______________________?

**b)** He isn't working today, ______________________?

**c)** Jermaine is reading, ______________________?

**d)** You can swim, ______________________?

**e)** She can't play the piano, ______________________?

## Activity 3

Draw a line to match the question tags to the sentences.

|  | |  |
|---|---|---|
| Jack's on holiday, | | shall we? |
| Let's go out tonight, | | isn't he? |
| Listen, | | will you? |
| Tom won't be late, | | will he? |
| You wouldn't tell anyone, | | would you? |

## Activity 4

Circle the questions that have question tags.

**a)** She is here, isn't she?

**b)** Where is the coat?

**c)** Is the dog in here?

**d)** That fish looks like a monster, doesn't it?

**e)** Don't you wish it was Monday?

## Investigate!

Can you find two different examples for each of the types of sentences in your school library?

Can you think of four sentences where you could use a question tag?

# 6 Expanded noun phrases

An **expanded noun phrase** is a group of words in a sentence that functions like a noun. An expanded noun phrase gives more information about the noun. We can add detail to a sentence by expanding the noun phrase. We can do this by adding an **adjective**, a **prepositional phrase** or **adverbial**.

**Eva** ate **the cake.**

**proper noun** (Eva) **noun phrase** (the cake)

Adding an adjective: Eva ate the **gooey chocolate** cake.

Adding a prepositional phrase: Eva ate the gooey chocolate cake **in the café**.

Adding an adverbial: **Yesterday,** Eva ate the gooey chocolate cake in the café.

## Activity 1

Complete the noun phrase table by adding a new word each time. The first one has been done for you.

a)

| | | | |
|---|---|---|---|
| | | | crocodile |
| | | green | crocodile |
| | | | |
| | | | |

b)

| | | | |
|---|---|---|---|
| | | | dog |
| | | | |
| | | | |
| | | | |

c)

| | | | |
|---|---|---|---|
| | | | motorbike |
| | | | |
| | | | |
| | | | |

## Activity 2

Underline the noun phrases in this text.

After preparing for an action-packed night outside, the excited, expectant faces of the children were lit by the glowing, luminous flames of the open fire. A pointed, sharp-beaked northern hawk owl gliding by produced shrill squeals that amazed the crowd.

## Activity 3

Look at the following passage. Modify the nouns in bold to improve the passage.

The **director** looked around the **theatre**.

"Which **actor** has left this **script**?"

"It's mine," said a **voice**.

"Come and read the **review**," said the **director**.

## Investigate!

Can you find examples in the school library of the different ways we can expand a noun to create an expanded noun phrase?

How can you use expanded noun phrases in your own writing? Look through a piece of work you have written recently and see if you could add a noun phrase.

# 7 Phrases and clauses

When learning about punctuation, it is helpful to understand the difference between a **phrase** and a **clause**.

| | | |
|---|---|---|
| **Phrase** | A group of words that may contains nouns or verbs but does not have a subject doing a verb. | some funny animals |
| **Clause** | A group of words that has a subject doing a verb. | some funny animals are running round the field |

## Activity 1

Tick the correct box to show if the group of words are phrases or clauses.

| | Phrase | Clause |
|---|---|---|
| at the bottom of the hill | | |
| the dog was very small | | |
| in a far-off and lonely village | | |
| Maya lived in a thatched cottage | | |
| the day before yesterday | | |

## Activity 2

Underline the clause in each of the sentences below. One has been done for you.

**a)** <u>She walked up the stairs</u>, laughing softly.

**b)** Before lunch, I will finish reading my book.

**c)** The sun was shining on the pitch, blinding the team.

**d)** Despite being dark and gloomy, the weather made him happy.

**e)** The dog, not altogether unsurprisingly, hates having a bath.

**f)** Over the fields and through the woods, the deer ran.

## Activity 3

Read the sentences below. Is the underlined section a phrase or a clause?

**a)** <u>Opening the gate</u>, Jose let his dog into the yard.

**b)** It is too bad <u>that Ms Fraser will not be teaching next year</u>.

**c)** The player <u>who hits the winning run</u> will be the player of the match.

**d)** The girl, <u>whose leg was broken last year</u>, will be running in the big race tomorrow.

**e)** After the game, <u>the team went out for ice-cream</u>.

**f)** Vicky's dog went missing <u>on the last stormy night</u>.

## Activity 4

Underline the phrase in each sentence. One has been done for you.

**a)** The sheep were led <u>to the field</u>.

**b)** Under the sea live all kinds of animals.

**c)** There is a gigantic spider under that chair.

**d)** Next year, we're going on an adventure!

**e)** Could you pass me the salt?

**f)** The enormous turnip grew rapidly!

**g)** Quickly hide the forbidden chocolate!

## Investigate!

Write a definition for a phrase and a clause to display around the classroom for others to use. Can you explain the difference between a phrase and a clause to a friend?

# 8 Subordinate clauses

**Subordinate clauses** are also called **independent clauses**. A subordinate clause starts with a **conjunction** and cannot stand alone as a sentence. A main clause and a subordinate clause go together to make a complex sentence.

**conjunction**

**I like the summer because I can go to the beach.**

**main clause** **subordinate clause**

Conjunctions include: while, because, although, where, until, if, though, when, since, so that, before, after, as, whenever.

## Activity 1

Underline the main clause in each of these sentences.

**a)** While looking through the window, Sophie saw the BFG.

**b)** Tom saw the maid when she came through the door.

**c)** Grandma said I could go down to the beach if I finished my homework.

**d)** Although it was late, Sean watched the film.

**e)** Mr Das bought the paper when he was on the train.

## Activity 2

Underline the subordinate clause in each of these sentences.

**a)** When he had finished washing the dishes, Lee sat down.

**b)** She felt sad whenever she saw the picture.

**c)** If you eat all your dinner, you can have an ice-cream.

**d)** Steven was brushing his teeth while his sister was brushing her hair.

**e)** Jay got a prize although he was last in the race.

## Activity 3

Use a conjunction to join each pair of clauses to make a complex sentence. Vary the sentence position of the conjunctions. Decide if a comma is needed and underline the subordinate clause. Remember to add full stops and capital letters where needed.

**a)** the school is popular
the Academy of Magic has many problems

______________________________

**b)** wizards are careless with potions
there are many mishaps

______________________________

**c)** I feel sick
I go on the boat

______________________________

## Activity 4

Write an independent clause to complete each of these sentences.

**a)** Unless you can do it faster, ______________________.

**b)** Sian went to school______________________.

**c)** Molly bought a birthday card______________________.

**d)** While you go to the river, ______________________.

**e)** I like the winter because ______________________.

## Investigate!

Can you explain the difference between a main clause and a subordinate clause?

Find three sentences in your reading book that contain a subordinate clause.

# 9 Active and passive voice

In an **active sentence**, the subject is doing the action.

The man drove the car.

In a **passive sentence**, the subject is having the action done to it.

The car was driven by the man.

## Activity 1

Decide whether each sentence is in the active or passive voice.

**a)** Mark was eating an apple. ____________________

**b)** The picture was painted by Isaac. ____________________

**c)** Tina opened the present. ____________________

**d)** The phone was being used by Mr Thomas. ____________________

**e)** The card was made by Fergus. ____________________

**f)** James hit the tree with his stick. ____________________

**g)** The man jumped off the step. ____________________

**h)** Daniel was watching the birds. ____________________

## Activity 2

These sentences are all written in the passive voice. Change each sentence into the active voice.

**a)** The football was kicked by Luke.

**b)** The knife was left on the table by Jade.

**c)** The milk had been knocked over by a cat.

**d)** The car had been driven into a wall by a teenager.

## Activity 3

Tick the correct column to show whether each sentence is written in the active voice or passive voice. One has been done for you.

**a)**

| | **Active voice** | **Passive voice** |
|---|---|---|
| All the lions were given their food at the same time. | | ✓ |
| Each of the elephants was sprayed with water by the keepers. | | |
| The tiger walked up and down the side of the enclosure. | | |

**b)**

| | **Active voice** | **Passive voice** |
|---|---|---|
| All of the children were given a special treat. | | |
| The window was broken by a stone. | | |
| Everyone was happy with the new play equipment. | | |

**c)**

| | **Active voice** | **Passive voice** |
|---|---|---|
| The winning song was sung by the boy band. | | |
| The bird carefully built the nest. | | |
| The toddler ripped the book in half. | | |

**d)**

| | **Active voice** | **Passive voice** |
|---|---|---|
| The parents watched their children in the play. | | |
| The question was answered by the teacher. | | |
| The fly was squashed by the chef. | | |

## Investigate!

Can you find some examples of the active voice and the passive voice in books that you have recently read.

Can you write or explain to a friend the difference between the active voice and passive voice?

# 10 Adverbials

An adverbial is a word or phrase that gives more information about a verb. Adverbs, prepositional phrases and subordinate phrases can all be used as adverbials. Adverbials answer questions such as **when, where, why, how** and **how often.**

| Type of adverbial | Question being answered | Examples | Adverbial in a sentence |
|---|---|---|---|
| Time | When? | after we had eaten dinner | We all played a game **after we had eaten dinner**. |
| Place | Where? | at the new ice-rink up the road | We went skating **at the new ice-rink up the road**. |
| Number | In what order? | first, second, once, last, twice, never | **First**, put the ingredients in a pan. |
| Frequency or degree | How did it happen? | very, extremely, until, quite, almost | We left **very** quietly.<br>There was an **extremely** large dog. |

## Activity 1

Underline the adverbials in these sentences.

**a)** Eleanor skipped down the road.

**b)** Jake laughed as soon as he opened the card.

**c)** We had curry and walked to the shops.

**d)** Before we went to school, we walked the dog.

**e)** The cat was asleep but I still didn't trust it.

**f)** The team were tired after they trained.

## Activity 2

Can you add an adverbial phrase to each of these sentences?

**a)** He threw the ball.

**b)** She dressed.

**c)** Her father fell.

**d)** His sister tried again.

**e)** He ate his vegetables.

## Activity 3

Tick the sentences where the underlined words are an adverbial.

**a)**

| | |
|---|---|
| We expect our grandparents to arrive in about an hour. | |
| My cousin watches television almost as much as you do. | |
| The weatherman says it will rain all day. | |
| Our friend drives on Mondays. | |
| The snake slithers through the tall grass. | |

**b)**

| | |
|---|---|
| He found his lucky penny in the morning. | |
| We raced our toy cars on the playground. | |
| The music teacher played the piano better than her student. | |
| Early in the morning the air is cold and fresh. | |
| Jan will run on the track at school. | |

**c)**

| | |
|---|---|
| I'll meet you outside the park gate. | |
| Can you meet me at 4pm? | |
| After you have watched the football, shall we get a drink? | |
| We hope to see you before the end of the week. | |
| More slowly than a worm, Donna made the cake. | |

## Investigate!

Can you find examples of different types of adverbials in the classroom?

How can you use adverbials in your own writing? Look through your writing and add adverbials to make your writing more interesting.

# Tense choice

Verbs can be written in the past, present or future tense.

- The **past tense** shows that something has already happened.
- The **present tense** shows that something is happening now.
- The **future tense** shows that something will happen after now.

## Activity 1

Complete the table below by inserting the correct tense of each verb.

| **Past tense (to sing)** | **Present tense (to wash)** | **Future tense (to eat)** |
|---|---|---|
| I sang | I | I |
| You | You | You |
| She | She washes | He |
| It | It | It |
| We | We | We will eat |
| They | They | They |

## Activity 2

Put each of these sentences into the past tense. (Some words may need to be changed or deleted to create the past tense.)

**a)** "I can't talk now; I'm just about to drive to Cardiff."

**b)** "This is the most exciting World Cup game I've ever seen."

**c)** "The suspect is now leaving the building via the underground car park."

**d)** "I'm finding it hard to breathe and I can't concentrate properly."

**e)** "She can't find the light switch and the room is in total darkness."

## Activity 3

Changing the tense from past to present can make things seem more real – as if they're happening now. Rewrite these sentences by putting them into the present tense.

**a)** I didn't know what was happening.

**b)** We had found her mobile phone in the cloakroom.

**c)** I had walked across the city all day looking for her.

**d)** The game finished.

**e)** I was having a lovely holiday.

**f)** She seemed to fly through the air during the gymnastic display.

## Activity 4

Write out a sentence for each of the following phrases. One should be written in the past tense, one in the present and one in the future.

**a)** watching a film at the cinema

______________________________

______________________________

**b)** being ill with flu

______________________________

______________________________

**c)** eating an expensive meal

______________________________

______________________________

## Investigate!

Can you find examples of an author writing using the different tense choices?

Can you find a paragraph where an author has written in the past tense and then change this to either the present or future tense?

# 12 Conjunctions

**Conjunctions** join clauses together. There are different types of conjunctions:

- Co-ordinating conjunctions – and, but, so

  You can run **or** you can hop.

- Subordinating conjunctions – because, as, so, if, although, despite, unless, when, after, while, before, where, once, during, until, since

  We can play in the garden **after** we eat our lunch.

## Activity 1

Underline the conjunction in each of these sentences.

**a)** This is Jack's new mountain bike, which he got from his parents. He locks it up every evening so that nobody can steal it.

**b)** Although my father loves jazz, he doesn't often listen to it.

**c)** While we were driving through the countryside, we saw lots of lovely villages.

**d)** Honda makes cars as well as motorcycles.

**e)** Our flight attendants must be able to speak both English and Spanish.

**f)** The weather was perfect as it was neither too hot nor too cold.

**g)** Lia invited me to her party last weekend, but I had to tell her I couldn't come.

**h)** I started to learn Italian during my stay in Rome.

## Activity 2

Circle the correct conjunction to complete each sentence.

**a)** Mum wanted a cup of tea ______ there was no milk.

**after** **before** **although** **during**

**b)** The dog chased the ball ______ hid it under his blanket.

**if** **and** **until** **before**

## Activity 3

Complete this text with the most suitable conjunction from the list below. Some of these conjunctions can be used more than once.

**with as after which while then although but**
**until causing because before or**

I flipped a coin into the air. It landed on its side _______________ rolled into the street, _______________ a bicycle to swerve dangerously. The rider fell off _______________ smashing into a fruit and vegetable stall, _______________ immediately collapsed. Turnips, carrots and potatoes rolled down the hill, _______________ I did my best to stop them _______________ I could see what was about to happen! A woman _______________ a heavy parcel was caught off balance _______________ the vegetables rolled around her feet _______________ she managed to stay standing – _______________ she was hit by an out-of-control parcel that fell through a pet shop window and scattered a litter of kittens, snakes and tarantulas. The woman ended up with a monkey on her head, waving its tail. That's the way with flipping a coin: you never know if it's going to be heads _______________ tails!

## Investigate!

How many conjunctions can you write in two minutes?

Use conjunctions from this unit in a wordsearch for others to complete.

# 13 Ellipsis

**Ellipsis** is where a word or a phrase is missing from writing but the context means the writing can still be understood. The plural of ellipsis is ellipses. An ellipsis sign is a set of three dots that shows words are missing.

**Reading as much as possible improves academic attainment.**
With an ellipsis this sentence becomes:
**Reading ... improves academic attainment.**

An ellipsis can also be used to show hesitation or an interruption in the idea being expressed to give a dramatic effect.

Shall I ... um ...?

Now then ... where was I?

## Activity 1

Write whether the ellipsis sign in these sentences shows hesitation (**H**), omitted words (**O**) or interruption (**I**).

**a)** Racing around the track, the athlete pulled ahead of his competitors ... and tripped.

**b)** He thought and thought … and thought.

**c)** After the incident on 18th May ... two teachers were injured.

**d)** "Can I just ...?" asked Jo tentatively.

## Activity 2

Cross out the words that are not needed or are repeated in these sentences. Can you insert ellipses or conjunctions to replace any of the missing words?

**a)** Mark really enjoyed the play; Lauren didn't really enjoy the play.

**b)** Smoking is bad for your health while exercise is good for your health.

**c)** We can jump over the river, swim over the river or fly over the river.

**d)** The pizza was tasty, the salad was tasty, the pasta was tasty.

**e)** Tina jumped in the pool; Jermaine jumped in the pool.

**f)** The football team flew over to America and won a major trophy.

## Activity 3

Rewrite each sentence below using an ellipsis.

**a)** I thought the party was nice.

______________________________

**b)** Otto said, "There's nothing inside."

______________________________

**c)** The dog looked at the large cat and then looked away.

______________________________

**d)** "I want," Stacy said, dreamily.

______________________________

**e)** "No, no, no, no!" exclaimed Horace.

______________________________

## Activity 4

Tick the sentences that have an ellipsis. If there is an ellipsis, write what the missing word(s) might be.

| Sentence | Ellipsis? | missing words |
|---|---|---|
| She ran the race … I didn't. | | |
| Ali walked to school … I did too. | | |
| The faster runners were Caitlin and Keira. | | |
| We went … Shazia stayed at home. | | |
| We don't, but Samsia does like to do maths. | | |

### Investigate!

Can you find three examples where an author has used an ellipsis in their writing?

Could you explain to a friend why and when to use an ellipsis correctly?

# 14 Formal and informal structures

Formal and informal styles must be chosen to suit the purpose of the writing.

- **Informal writing** is personal and chatty. (Used in a letter to a friend, such as **I am writing to ask...**)
- **Formal writing** is impersonal and uses the third person. (Used in a letter of complaint, such as **I am writing to enquire...**)

Note: the third person represents everyone and everything else, and uses the singular pronouns **he** and **him**, **she** and **her**, and **it**, and then the plural pronouns **they** and **them**.

she sings, they sing

## Activity 1

Can you think of a formal way of saying these words or phrases?

**a)** cash

**b)** Phone you back

**c)** Get your money back

**d)** letters

**e)** granny

**f)** kid

## Activity 2

Rewrite this text using formal language.

It was sort of dark in the house, and kind of smelly too. We raised a right din racing up the stairs. The gang and me'd played there all day, 'cos Dad said it were ok.

## Activity 3

Write these contractions or abbreviations in full.

a) it's ____________

b) e.g. ____________

c) she'll ____________

d) & ____________

e) approx ____________

f) RU OK? ____________

**Remember!**

**Formal language tends not to use abbreviations and contractions but informal language does.**

## Activity 4

Use a thesaurus to find a more formal option for these informal words.

a) cool

b) said

c) good

d) get

e) great

f) telly

## Investigate!

Can you list examples of when you would write with an informal style and a formal style?

# 15 Subject and verb agreement

A singular **subject** works with a singular verb.

The box is ready.

In the example, **box** is the singular subject and **is** is the singular verb.

A plural subject works with a plural verb.

The children have arrived.

In the example, **children** is the plural subject and **have** is the plural verb.

## Activity 1

Circle the verbs that need changing in these sentences.

**a)** We was at school when the police car arrived.

**b)** The children always slides on the grass.

**c)** Jake and Ben was pleased to get a day off school.

**d)** If Jamal or Cody are early, ask them to help you.

**e)** Greg and the girls rides every Wednesday night.

## Activity 2

Underline the correct word to complete the sentences below.

**a)** Margo and her parents (visit/visits) each other often.

**b)** Either the cups or the glasses (is/are) in the dishwasher.

**c)** Vern and Fred (need/needs) a ride to work.

**d)** Our team (is/are) trying hard to win a medal.

**e)** Neither Matt nor his brothers (was/were) at the party.

## Activity 3

**a)** Which sentence shows the correct agreement between the subject and verb?

| | Tick **one** |
|---|---|
| The walkers carries their lunch in their backpacks. | |
| They eats all the pudding. | |
| The baker makes gorgeous cakes. | |
| He go to the dentist twice a year. | |

**b)** Which sentence shows the correct agreement between the subject and verb?

| | Tick **one** |
|---|---|
| Many of my friends loves eating pizza. | |
| Everyone is going to the library. | |
| The man live near the station. | |
| The boys is sitting in the classroom. | |

## Activity 4

Complete each sentence correctly by filling in the gap with **talk** or **talks**.

**a)** If Joe or Yani ______, send them to the head teacher.

**b)** The teachers and the parents ______ about us far too often!

**c)** Eva and Tia always ______ too much at bedtime.

**d)** The commentator ______ to the manager after each game.

**e)** "Come and ______ to me at the end of the lesson, please," said the teacher.

**f)** The parents ______ a lot before the school performance.

**g)** Mum often ______ about her family in Poland.

## Investigate!

Explain and write the rules for subject and verb agreement to display around the classroom.

Can you find examples in books you have read where there is subject and verb agreement?

# 16 Subject, object and verb

To understand sentences, you need to be able to identify the main parts: the **subject**, **verb** and **object**.

Subject – tells you who or what does the action.

Object – is who or what the action is done to.

The **dog** **chased** the **cat**.

subject (dog) verb (chased) object (cat)

## Activity 1

Underline the subject and the object in each sentence in different colours.

**a)** The dog runs around the field wildly.

**b)** Dad bought a new car.

**c)** My teddy fell off the bed.

**d)** I walk away from the building.

**e)** The ring glittered on my finger.

**f)** George jumps over the gate every morning.

**g)** Melanie watched a sad film.

**h)** The teacher gave the pupil a gold star.

**i)** I bought a present for my sister.

**j)** The paper boy delivers my newspaper late most days.

## Activity 2

Write a sentence using the subject, object and verb that are given in each row.

| subject | object | verb |
|---|---|---|
| bus | wall | drove |
| squid | diver | squirted |
| computer | robot | controlled |
| candle | fire | started |
| dog | lead | fetched |

## Activity 3

Underline the verb in **blue**, circle the subject in **red** and highlight the object in **yellow**.

**a)** Matt tidied his bedroom. He washed up the breakfast things. He had forgotten to buy a present. It was Mother's Day.

**b)** I have flu. I have all of the usual symptoms. I have a sore throat. The room is cold. I don't feel like eating anything.

**c)** Sarah was nervous. It was her first day at her new school. She knew nobody. It was a huge building. Sarah had a different teacher for every lesson and it was very confusing.

## Activity 4

Choose the correct sentence each time.

**a)** Circle the sentence where the subject is the dog.

The man saw the dogs.

The dogs barked at the man.

**b)** Circle the sentence where the object is the cake.

The cake was for my birthday.

Jordan ate the cake.

**c)** Circle the sentence where the subject is the car.

The car was a Ferrari.

The winner was the car.

## Investigate!

Read a paragraph from your reading book. Can you write down the subject, object and verb in each sentence?

Can you explain the difference between the subject, object and verb to a friend?

# 17 Is and are

**Is** and **are** are forms of the verb **to be**. There are some simple rules to follow that will help you decide if you need to use **is** or **are**.

**Is** is singular: use **is** if you are talking about only one person, but not yourself (for that you use **am**).

- **He is** about to go the park.
- **She is** about to go to the park.
- **Sasha** is about to go to the park.

**Are** is plural: use **are** for more than one person including you.

- **We are** going to the park.
- **You are** going to the park.

## Activity 1

Choose whether to use **is** or **are** in the following sentences.

**a)** At the moment, the queen is/are in the kitchen.

**b)** She is/are a good cook.

**c)** The king is/are no good with tools.

**d)** The queen and king is/are sleeping at home.

**e)** They is/are looking forward to a relaxing day tomorrow.

**f)** The queen is/are painting and the king is/are poaching eggs.

## Activity 2

Use **is** or **are** to complete the sentences below.

**a)** ____________ you having fun on the bouncy castle?

**b)** He ____________ coming to my party.

**c)** The boys ____________ jumping on the bed.

**d)** ____________ you going out for a meal tonight?

**e)** Why ____________ they so mad at me?

**f)** What ____________ she doing now?

## Activity 3

Write **is** or **are** in the blanks below.

**a)** There ________ many animals in the zoo.

**b)** There ________ a snake in the window.

**c)** There ________ a zebra in the grass.

**d)** There ________ lions in the zoo, too.

**e)** There ________ some young lions with their mothers.

**f)** There ________ a bird next to the tree.

**g)** There ________ many monkeys in the trees.

**h)** There ________ an elephant in the zoo.

## Activity 4

Can you find the mistakes in the text and write a correct version? Look out for the incorrect use of **is** or **are**, and check for the incorrect use of the singular and plural forms of different verbs.

Norwich is a 'fine city' according to the signs that welcomes you as you arrives on the city outskirts. There is interesting city walks through the old, narrow streets and by the river, and there is many medieval buildings. Boat trips regularly leaves the city to join the River Yare into the famous Norfolk Broads. There are man-made waterways that covers much of east Norfolk to the coast.

Thousands of visitors comes to Norwich every year. They enjoys exploring the city, which have many old buildings, some of which dates back hundreds of years. The Castle stand on a mound and now serve as the region's principal museum, with a variety of displays.

The most famous building, however, are the cathedral, which lie off an attractive street, Tombland. The spire of the cathedral dominate the city: only the city of Salisbury have a higher spire.

## Investigate!

Can you write down the rules for using **is** and **are** to display around the classroom? Teach a friend from Year 5 the rules.

Look back through your writing. Have you used **is** and **are** correctly?

# 18 Colons

A **colon** can be used in different ways.

- To introduce a list, an example, playscript or a quotation.
- To separate two independent clauses where the second clause expands on or illustrates the first.

However, the colon must always be preceded by a full sentence.

There were many precious items in the treasure chest: gold, rubies, pearls and crystals.

The treasure chest was precious: full of gold and other expensive jewels.

## Activity 1

Add a colon to each of these sentences.

**a)** I eat lots of fruit bananas, pears and apples.

**b)** My wardrobe is full of clothes jumpers, jeans, socks and shirts.

**c)** There were many beautiful items of jewellery necklaces, bracelets, rings and earrings.

**d)** We have plenty to do on our camping trip build tents, make fires, clean dishes and cook the food.

## Activity 2

Where should the colon go in each of these sentences? Write the correct sentences.

**a)** He quoted the famous speech To be or not to be.

**b)** My friends think I'm funny I make them laugh, play tricks and tell jokes.

**c)** Jill had to answer the question yes or no.

**d)** Don't forget the number one class rule raise your hand.

## Investigate!

Can you write down the different times you would use a colon in your writing?

Show how you would use a colon in fiction and non-fiction writing.

# 19 Semi-colons

A **semi-colon** is used to separate two complete sentences that are very closely related but should not be joined with a colon.

Susan was warm; the sunshine was pleasant.

There needs to be a complete sentence both before and after the semicolon, but don't use a capital letter for the second sentence.

## Activity 1

Rewrite these sentences using a semi-colon to replace the conjunction.

**a)** It was a cold day so I had to wrap up warmly.

**b)** I felt really silly because I got the answer wrong.

**c)** Our dogs race around the field because they are very energetic animals.

**d)** The thief escaped because he fought his way through the crowd.

**e)** I liked the book as it was a pleasure to read.

**f)** The first film was the best because I thought the sequel was rubbish.

**g)** I switched off the alarm clock as it was time to get up.

**h)** I ran some cold water into the bath because it was far too hot.

## Activity 2

Where should the semi-colon be used in these sentences?

**a)** There was an accident at the front of the school the teachers all went out to help.

**b)** I have found a brilliant book I can't stop reading it.

**c)** The explorer discovered a new plant it was named after her.

**d)** They climbed to the top of the mountain the view was amazing.

## Investigate!

Can you explain how to use a semi-colon? Write the rules and give an example in a sentence?

Have a look through your reading book and find examples of where an author has used a semi-colon.

# Inverted commas

**Inverted commas** (“ and ”) are also called speech marks. They are placed around the words that are spoken. Each pair of inverted commas is preceded by either a new line or punctuation such as a **full stop**, **comma**, **question mark** or **exclamation mark**.

“Would you like to come round for a cup of tea?” asked Ian.

Maddie replied, “Yes, that would be lovely.”

## Activity 1

Insert the missing inverted commas in the sentences below.

**a)** If you head west from Ireland, said the tour guide, you'll eventually get to America.

**b)** Excuse me, whispered Claire. I am feeling extremely nervous about my performance. Do you have any tips for me, please?

**c)** First fill the jelly mould, said the chef. Then place it in the fridge to chill.

**d)** When you reach the end of the road, said the police officer, you should turn left.

**e)** Here is your maths homework, said the teacher. Please return it next Thursday.

**f)** Why haven't you tidied your bedroom? asked Mum. You said that you would do it yesterday.

## Activity 2

Rewrite this sentence, adding inverted commas.

Why didn't I think of that! she exclaimed as she watched her brother solve the puzzle. It was easy!

________________________________________

________________________________________

## Activity 3

**a)** Which of the following sentences uses inverted commas correctly?

| | Tick **one** |
|---|---|
| "So when he entered your shop, said the detective, he stole some computer games." | |
| "So when he entered your shop," said the detective, he stole some computer games. | |
| "So when he entered your shop," said the detective, "he stole some computer games." | |
| So when he entered your shop, said the detective, "he stole some computer games." | |

**b)** Which of the following sentences uses inverted commas correctly?

| | Tick **one** |
|---|---|
| "Can you help me please?" asked the girl. "I am lost." | |
| "Can you help me please? asked the girl, I am lost." | |
| Can you help me please? "asked the girl," I am lost. | |
| Can you help me please? asked the girl, "I am lost." | |

**c)** Which of the following sentences uses inverted commas correctly?

| | Tick **one** |
|---|---|
| "Follow me shouted the teacher." | |
| "Follow me," shouted the teacher. | |
| "Follow me. "shouted the teacher." | |
| "Follow me," "shouted the teacher." | |

**d)** Which of the following sentences uses inverted commas correctly?

| | Tick **one** |
|---|---|
| Can I have a cake please? asked Billy, "I'm starving." | |
| "Can I have a cake please? asked Billy, I'm starving." | |
| "Can I have a cake please?" asked Billy. "I'm starving." | |
| "Can I have a cake please?" "asked Billy," "I'm starving." | |

### Investigate!

Write down the rules for using inverted commas to display in the classroom. Look back through your writing and check to see if you have followed the rules for adding inverted commas.

# 21 Bullet points

**Bullet points** are used to draw attention to important information in a document so that a reader can identify the key issues and facts quickly. There are two types of bulleted lists: **ordered** and **unordered**.

| An **ordered** list means that a list is numbered. | An **unordered** list means that a list is not numbered. |
|---|---|
| 1. | • |
| 2. | • |
| 3. | • |

There are two ways you can punctuate bullet points correctly.

- If the bulleted items are not full sentences, they can begin with a lower-case letter. The list will usually have a colon at the end of the previous sentence.

You will need:

- some paper
- a paintbrush
- some paints.

The last item in the list will need a full stop.

- If the bulleted items are complete sentences, each one needs to begin with a capital letter and end with a full stop, question mark or exclamation mark.

## Activity 1

Read the following text about penguins. Use bullet points to identify the main facts. You may need to reword some parts of the text.

**Why Emperor Penguins do not feel the cold**

All animals that live in very cold climates, such as polar bears, arctic foxes and seals, have large bodies and small feet, wings or, in the case of penguins, small flippers. By keeping their flippers close to the body, it is easier to keep warm. Penguins have an amazing number of feathers (approximately ten feathers per square centimetre), which are packed tightly together, acting as an insulating layer, holding in body heat and making them waterproof.

The Emperor Penguin's nose is very well adapted to the cold. The chambers in their noses reuse much of the heat that is normally lost during breathing out. Another special adaptation of the Emperor Penguin is the ability to 'recycle' its own body heat. The Emperor's arteries and veins that carry blood around the body to the extremities lie close together so that blood is cooled on the way to the bird's feet, wings and bill and warmed on the way back to the heart.

Emperor Penguins have large layers of energy-giving body fat called blubber. They are not very active during winter so they don't use up the fat. They are also very social creatures, which means they congregate in large groups, and one of their survival tactics is to huddle together to keep warm. This huddling instinct means that they do not lose much heat when they are inside the huddle because they insulate each other.

## Activity 2

Write an ordered list of the equipment you would need for the following tasks.

**a)** making a cup of tea

**b)** baking a cake

**c)** going swimming

**d)** getting ready for school

**e)** cleaning a car

## Investigate!

Find two non-fiction texts from the school library. Write down, using bullet points, the main facts you have found out about each text.

# 22 Hyphens

Hyphens are short dashes between two words.

father-in-law

Hyphens have many uses.

Hyphens can be used to make compound nouns that are used as adjectives.

**well-dressed man, hang-gliding professional**

They can make a verb from two nouns.

**to test-drive**

Hyphens are used to add a prefix to some words.

**re-examine, ex-wife**

## Activity 1

Can you match the hyphenated words to their meanings?

| | |
|---|---|
| football-mad | someone who is good at gardening |
| green-fingered | someone who loves football |
| level-headed | a person who likes sweet things |
| clean-shaven | a sensible person who thinks carefully |
| sweet-toothed | someone who's just had a shave |

## Activity 2

Can you write a sentence for each of the words in the list below?

**animal-lover** **tongue-tied** **monster-like** **fair-haired** **sweet-smelling**

**a)** ____________________

**b)** ____________________

**c)** ____________________

**d)** ____________________

**e)** ____________________